Dom Helder Câmara was ordained in
1931, and served as auxiliary bishop of
Rio de Janeiro from 1952 to 1964. He was
then made archbishop of Olinda and Re-
cife in North-East Brazil, the poorest and
least developed region of the country.

In a larger sense, he is the bishop of
all those everywhere who share his conviction that inhuman structures can be
changed by the violence of truth and justice.

THE DESERT
IS FERTILE

Dom Helder Câmara

Translated by
Dinah Livingstone

ORBIS BOOKS
MARYKNOLL   NEW YORK

THE DESERT IS FERTILE

Published by Pillar Books for Orbis Books

Paperback edition published January 1976

ISBN: 0-88344-078-4

Library of Congress Catalog Card Number: 73-89315

Originally published as *Le desert est fertile* by Desclée de Brouwer, Editeurs SA, Brussels

English translation copyright © 1974 Orbis Books

Printed in the United States of America

Orbis Books
Maryknoll, New York 10545

CONTENTS

1

A FORCE LIKE NUCLEAR ENERGY

1 The lesson of half-failure

The world is so complicated that it would be ridiculous to try and produce a formula applicable to all situations, races, countries and continents. But there are problems overriding this diversity which face humanity as a whole, although of course they occur in varying forms and degrees.

Is there anywhere in the world free from injustice, inequality and division? Is there anywhere where injustice is not the primary violence breeding all other violence? Where violent protest against injustice, taking to the streets, does not threaten public order and the security of the state? And where it does not meet with violent repression by the authorities?

Almost everywhere there are many, particularly among the young, who have come to believe that the only way to do away with injustice is to rouse the victims of injustice, the oppressed, and organise them to fight for better days.

There are also many who want a juster and more human world but do not believe that force and armed violence are the best way of getting it. Those who choose active non-violence—the violence of the peaceful—do not need religion or ideology to see that the earth is ruled today by powerful combines, economic, political, technocratic and military alliances. How would it be possible to beat these lords of the earth in armed combat when they have as their allies arms manufacturers and war-mongers?

The difficult question then arises: what can be achieved by non-violence? Do the non-violent realise that the need is not just for a few small reforms but, in both the developed and the under-developed countries, the transformation of the political, cultural, economic and social structures?

Yes. The non-violent do not in the least underestimate the difficulty of the task. If I may speak personally, I could mention my own half-failure, which forces me to struggle on and offers me new hopes.

I dreamt for six years of a large liberating moral pressure movement. I started Action for Justice and Peace. I travelled half the world. I appealed to institutions, universities, churches, religious groups, trade unions, technicians' organisations, youth movements, etc. After six years I concluded that institutions as such are unable to engage in bold and decisive action for two reasons: they can only interpret the average opinions of their members, and in capitalist society they have to be directly or indirectly bound up with the system in order to survive.

Of course I was not able to visit the Eastern blocs. But if we condemn the serious failings in the capitalist super-states like the US and the EEC, we must likewise condemn the communist super-states, the USSR and China. And although it is still possible to denounce these failings in capitalist countries, it is not possible in Moscow or Peking.

And although I now realise that it is virtually useless to appeal to institutions as such, everywhere I go—and

8

intuitively I include the East—I find minorities with the power for love and justice which could be likened to nuclear energy locked for millions of years in the smallest atoms and waiting to be released.

But before I say who and where these minorities are, and what they can do together, let us agree as brothers on the ideas I am about to put forward, and the words I shall use.

We bless you Father

We bless you Father,
for the thirst
you put in us,
for the boldness
you inspire,
for the fire
alight in us,
that is you in us,
you the just.

Never mind
that our thirst
is mostly unquenched
(pity the satisfied).
Never mind
our bold plots
are mostly unclinched,
wanted not realised.

Who better than you
knows that success
comes not from us.
You ask us to do
our utmost only,
but willingly.

2 A marvellous discovery

The essential thing is this marvellous discovery: that all over the world, among all races, languages, religions, ideologies, there are men and women born to serve their neighbour, ready for any sacrifice if it helps to build at last a really juster and more human world.

They belong in their own environment but they feel themselves to be members of the human family. They think of other people everywhere as their brothers and sisters, people from every latitude and longitude, every climate, people of all sizes and colours, rich or poor, whatever their education or their culture.

I beg you, let us try and understand this message with all good will. Let every minority make it its own and translate it into its own language.

I am from the west, a Latin American, a christian. That is the language in which I clothe my thoughts and I shall not change it. If you do not believe in God, do not be irritated when I refer to him, or to Christ, if you are not a christian. Translate into your own language the truths I speak which are not the creations of personal fantasy but realities experienced together by all those who belong to the same spiritual family.

Sometimes the text will suggest simple translations, simplified because we have decided to unite, knowing the time is short and the severe problems we face are daily becoming more severe. I will set out simply how I see our minorities, and why I think they have essential work to do in the unification of mankind and the establishment of lasting peace through love and justice.

Lord save me

Lord save me
from the false centre.
In particular
defend me
from self-centredness.

Can we not realise
finally—now
let us not lack
understanding—
that without you,
we and everything
must be eccentric.

3 First, Abraham

God could have chosen many ways of sharing out his
gifts. He could have shared them out with strict equali-
ty. No one would have reason for complaint, no one
would have more or less. Everything would have been
calculated, adjusted, balanced . . .

But this would be unworthy of the Father's creative
imagination. It would be incredibly monotonous, as if
all human beings had exactly the same face, or all
flowers were the same shape and colour and smelt the
same . . .

God accepts the risk of appearing to be unjust. At

least he does not refuse anyone the indispensable. But some have gifts heaped upon them. I am speaking here of true riches, the riches of the personality. There are people who are rich in divine gifts and privileged by divine grace.

God looks unjust but he is not. He asks more from those to whom he gives more. They are not greater or better, they have greater responsibility. They must give more service. Live to serve.

Some people will now hurriedly insist—but without great conviction or sincerity—that they have barely the essentials etc. But it is a waste of time to weigh up and measure gifts in this way. It is not important whether we have been given much or little. What matters is to make a firm decision to make the best possible use of them and to serve.

God thinks of all men but calls some to special work. He drives these to take a leap in the dark, to set out. He tries them by fearful hardships. But he supports and encourages them. He gives them the fine and dangerous mission to act as his instruments. He entrusts them with the task of being present discreetly when decisive decisions are made. He sends them out on the road to draw others to them, many others. He expects them to bear witness in the hour of trial.

Abraham was the first to be thus called by God. He did not delay for a moment. He set out. He faced hardships. He learned to his cost how to arouse his brothers in the name of God. To call. To encourage. To start moving.

Jews, christians and muslims know the story of the father of believers. What is his name in the other great religions?

Did Abraham receive great gifts? He gave a faithful return, the best he could. He served.

Will those who are not Jews or christians or muslims

13

allow us to give Abraham's name to those minorities who are called to serve? Of course other races and religions can use an equivalent name which is more appropriate to their tradition.

And you my brothers who are atheist humanists, don't think you have been forgotten. Translate what I say in my language into your language. When I talk of God, translate, perhaps by 'nature', 'evolution', what you will.

If you feel in you the desire to use the qualities you have, if you think selfishness is narrow and choking, if you hunger for truth, justice and love, you can and should go with us. Even if you don't know it, or perhaps don't want to know, you are our brother or sister. Accept our friendship. We will learn to understand each other and we will be able to go forward together.

Have you noticed who bury their talents?

Not just the man with only one,
but people given five or ten,
instead of reaping double,
become comfortable,
falsely cautious,
falsely humble,
and at harvest home return
in empty-handed barrenness.
Don't call them yet to account.
Wait a moment.
Let me go out
to my brothers, try
to rouse them by my cry.

Hope without risk

Hope without risk
is not hope,
which is believing
in risky loving,
trusting others
in the dark,
the blind leap
letting God take over.

From the jugful

From the jugful,
one drop alone
was called to share
in the sacrifice.
Why this
and not another?
Who can see,
who understands?
This placid water
moved me.
It was humble
and content a moment later
to wash clean
my unclean hands.

4 The global scale

Mankind's inclination towards laziness, avarice and comfort is well known.

We are told that we only use a tenth of our brains. What about the earth? It is startling to compare the cultivated and uncultivated areas. We are not talking about the sea, the air or light. Knowledge and use of these resources are still at the stage of pre-history. We are still only on the threshold of space travel, which will open thousands of worlds to us . . .

Men do not work as hard as they could in their daily life either. We are not condemning rest. Or recommending an inhuman activism which allows for no leisure, meetings, conversations.

But since we are called to live more generously, born to serve others, to rouse them, to belong to the family of Abraham, it is impossible for us to be happy and peaceful if we do not respond 100 per cent to the gifts we have been given.

It is important to fight against selfishness. Sometimes we are discouraged. Then we have the feeling that there is no point in thinking about others, that it would be better to renounce our ideals and be practical, looking after ourselves alone. Experience shows that selfishness is certain to bring unhappiness to ourselves and to others. We must struggle on with the determination to keep our hearts and minds wide open.

It is right and proper that we should have a particular love of our 'immediate family', the human group which gave us life. Whatever conditions you live in, care for you and yours but refuse to be locked within the narrow circle of your immediate family. Decide to take on the whole family of mankind.

It is also right and proper that we should have a particular love for our country, race, religion, mother tongue. But in loving your country and your own cultural environment, try not to feel a stranger anywhere else in the world. Be a man among men. Do not be indifferent to anyone's problems. Make the sufferings and humiliations of all your brothers your own. Live on a global scale, or better still take the whole universe.

You understand the meaning of the word 'pusillanimous'. It means someone who has a small mean soul. 'Magnanimous' is the opposite, and means great of soul, great hearted.

In your thoughts, your wishes and your actions try to be truly great hearted. Cross out words like *enemy, hostility, hatred, resentment, grudge,* from your dictionary . . .

One more piece of advice. It is a poor man who believes in his own worth, who thinks of himself as bold and lucid and better than other men. He who has received the most is the poorest. If he was given so much, this was because he did not have strength and value in himself. And if he has received much he has a moral obligation to think of others and to serve them. Serve them to the utmost.

King's son

Lord,
isn't your creation wasteful?
Fruits never equal
the seedlings' abundance.
Springs scatter water.
The sun gives out
enormous light.
May your bounty teach me
greatness of heart.
May your magnificence
stop me being mean.
Seeing you a prodigal
and open-handed giver,
let me give unstintingly,
like a king's son,
like God's own.

5 God's voice today

We are told that Abraham and other patriarchs heard
the voice of God. Can we also hear the Lord's call?
Isn't it pretentious to say this? Dangerously presump-
tuous?

We live in a world where millions of our fellow men
live in inhuman conditions, practically in slavery. If we
are not deaf we hear the cries of the oppressed. Their
cries are the voice of God.

We who live in rich countries where there are always
pockets of under-development and wretchedness, hear
if we want to hear, the unvoiced demands of those who

have no voice and no hope. The pleas of those who have no voice and no hope are the voice of God.

Anyone who has become aware of the injustices caused by the unfair division of wealth, must, if he has a heart, listen to the silent or violent protests of the poor. The protests of the poor are the voice of God. If we look at the relations between the poor countries and the capitalist and communist empires, we see that today injustice is not only done by one man to another, or by one group to another, but by one country to another. And the voice of the countries suffering these injustices is the voice of God.

In order to rouse us God makes use even of radical and violent rebellion. How can we not feel the urgent need to act when we see young people—sincere in their desire to fight injustice, but with violent means which only call down violent repression—show such courage in prison and under torture that it is difficult to believe that they are sustained only by materialist ideals. He who has eyes to see and ears to hear must feel challenged: how can we remain mediocre and ineffective when we have our faith to sustain us?

Are we so deaf that we do not hear a loving God warning us that humanity is in danger of committing suicide? Are we so selfish that we do not hear the just God demanding that we do all we can to stop injustice suffocating the world and driving it to war? Are we so alienated that we can worship God at our ease in luxurious temples which are often empty in spite of all their liturgical pomp, and fail to see, hear and serve God where he is present and where he requires our presence, among mankind, the poor, the oppressed, the victims of injustices in which we ourselves are often involved?

It is not difficult to hear God's call today in the world about us. It is difficult to do more than offer an emotional response, sorrow and regret. It is even more difficult to give up our comfort, break with old habits, let ourselves be moved by grace and change our life, be converted.

Come Lord

Do not smile and say
you are already with us.
Millions do not know you
and to us who do,
what is the difference?
What is the point of your presence
if our lives do not alter?
Change our lives, shatter
our complacency.
Make your word
flesh of our flesh,
blood of our blood
and our life's purpose.
Take away the quietness
of a clear conscience.
Press us uncomfortably.
For only thus
that other peace is made,
your peace.

6 Setting out on the road . . .

Setting out is first of all getting out of ourself. Breaking through the shell of selfishness hardening us within our own ego.

To stop revolving round ourself as if we were the centre of everything.

Refusing to be ringed in by the problems of our own small world. However important these may be, mankind is more important and our task is to serve mankind.

Setting out is not covering miles of land or sea, or travelling faster than the speed of sound. It is first and foremost opening ourselves to other people, trying to get to know them, going out to meet them.

Opening ourselves to ideas, including those with which we disagree, this is what the good traveller should do. Happy are they who understand the words 'If you disagree with me you have something to give me'.

If those who are with you always agree with you before you open your mouth, they are not companions but shadows. When disagreement is not a form of systematic blocking, when it rises from a different vision, it can only enrich us.

It is possible to travel alone. But the good traveller knows that the journey is human life and life needs company. 'Companion' means, etymologically, he who eats the same bread. Happy are they who feel they are always on the road and that every man they meet is their chosen companion. The good traveller takes care of his weary companions. He guesses when they lose heart. He takes them as he finds them, listens to them. Intelligently, gently, above all lovingly, he encourages them to go on and recover their joy in the journey.

To travel for the sake of travelling is not the true journey. We must seek a goal, envisage an end to the journey, an arrival.

But there are journeys and journeys. For the Abrahamic minorities, setting out means to get moving and help many others get moving to make the world juster and more human.

If you disagree with me

If you disagree with me,
you have something to give me,
if you are sincere
and seek the truth
as best you may,
honestly, with modest care,
your thought is growth
to mine, correction,
you deepen my vision.

You are hemmed in

If you want to be free of yourself
you must build a bridge over the gulf
of loneliness your selfishness
has found, and look beyond.
Listen to another,
and especially,
try loving him or her
and not just 'me'.

You want to be

You want to be,
excuse me,
first get free
of that excess
of goods
which cram
your whole body
leaving no room
for you and even less
for God.

7 The inevitable desert

We must have no illusions. We must not be naïve. If
we listen to the voice of God, we make our choice, get
out of ourselves and fight non-violently for a better
world. We must not expect to find it easy; we shall not
walk on roses, people will not throng to hear us and
applaud, and we shall not always be aware of divine
protection. If we are to be pilgrims for justice and
peace, we must expect the desert.

The great and the powerful disappear, stop helping
us and turn against us. They finance campaigns which
become shriller with lies the closer they feel the danger
coming. And what is worse, those who are not powerful also avoid us. They are frightened. Someone who
depends entirely on the boss for housing, work and
livelihood, is afraid of losing them for himself and
especially his family. His natural and understandable
reaction is to run away. There are others who are less

dependent on the rich, or more aware of the situation, who are ready for anything.

There are times when we look about us and feel we are an awkward friend. People who welcome us are suspect. They want our friendship but they are afraid of being compromised by our reputation.

We feel we are speaking in a desert, as did all those who were active in the cause of justice before us. Injustice spreads and becomes worse. It has two thirds of the earth in its grip. Only the stones listen. Or men with hearts of stone.

Our weariness spreads from the body to the soul. Which is worse than any bodily exhaustion.

We feel the desert round us as far as our eyes can see. Soft sand which we sink in up to our knees. Blinding and burning sand storms, which hurt our face, get in our eyes and ears . . .

We reach the limit of endurance, desert all about us, desert within. We feel that the Father himself has abandoned us. 'Why hast thou forsaken me?' . . .

We must not trust in our own strength, we must not give way to bitterness, we must stay humble knowing that we are in the hands of God, we must want only to share in the making of a better world. Then we shall not lose our courage or our hope. We shall feel the invisible protection of God our Father.

Lord guide me

If you try me,
send me out
into the foggy night,
so that I cannot see
my way.
Even if I stumble,
this I beg, that I
may look and smile
serenely,
bearing witness
that you are with me
and I walk in peace.

If you try me,
send me out
into an atmosphere
too thin for me to breathe
and I cannot feel the earth
beneath my feet,
let my behaviour
show men that they cannot
part me forcibly
from you in whom we
breathe and move
and are.

If you let hate
hamper and trap me,
twist my heart,
disfigure me,
then give my eyes
his love and peace,
my face the expression
of your Son.

8 The secret of eternal youth

The secret of remaining young, even when the years have changed our bodies, is to devote our life to a cause. At twenty, even without a wrinkle or a single grey hair, it is possible to be beaten by life, to be an old pessimist! They who do not understand what life is about or what they should do with it, risk losing their youth . . .

It is important to devote our life to a cause. But it is also important not to choose the wrong cause. History gives examples of great causes.

Countries like Brazil suffered for centuries the shame of African slavery. We can understand the enthusiasm of the young for the abolitionist movement. They cheerfully took great risks to help the slaves gain their freedom, and to arouse public opinion to destroy the structures which allowed slavery to exist. Poets, journalists, lawyers, priests, every sort of men and women joined together to fight for freedom for all God's children.

In Latin America in the nineteenth century, and in Asia and Africa in the twentieth century, arose the anti-colonialist movement to support people in their struggle for political independence. The world understood that it would be shameful and useless to try and preserve these colonialist structures. Every liberated country has its own heroes, poets, speakers, martyrs, saints.

Without underestimating other causes worthy of devotion and sacrifice, we can say confidently that today there is one cause which is the most important in our century, to free those two out of every three men who are still in slavery, even if they are no longer called slaves. To complete the liberation of countries who may have gained their political independence but must still gain economic independence, without which even their entry into the United Nations does not mean very much. The great thing is that this time, the effort must be made by all men and for all men.

Become an expert

Become an expert
in the art
of discovering the good
in every person.
No one
is entirely bad.
Become an expert
in the art
of finding the truthful core
in views of every kind.
The human mind
abhors total error.

Do not fear the truth

Do not fear the truth,
hard as it may appear,
grievously as it may hurt,
it is still right
and you were born for it.
If you go out to meet
and love it,
let it exercise your mind,
it is your best friend
and closest sister.

To the end

No, do not give in.
Grace divine
was your good beginning.
That grace is greater
which does not falter.
But the greatest
is to keep going
however
you are undermined,
to endure,
however harassed
to the end.

2

THIS CENTURY'S GREAT CAUSE

1 The root of evil

When we try to find the root of evil and ask what is the greatest problem of this century and the greatest danger to humanity, we find that for many people, this evil of evils is communism.

Of course we should not forget that Soviet Russia and Red China not only preach dialectical materialism but wish to impose it by force on the world without any qualms about crushing people and nations who dare to disagree with them.

But it is also true, and this many people do not know or forget, perhaps because it suits them to forget, that capitalism which holds itself up as the defender of the free world and higher values, also has materialist roots. Many people also do not know or conveniently forget that today there are socialist systems which do not support dialectical materialism and which, at least in theory, respect the rights of individuals.

History shows—the Yalta pact for example at the end of the second world war—that common interests are stronger than ideological differences, that capitalist and communist superpowers can get on beautifully if they wish to. The USSR and Red China are as imperialist as the US. The US and Soviet Russia have been equally indifferent to problems of trade and development at the United Nations Conference. When China joins the UN and takes part in these meetings it will behave in the same way.

We should also mention that the US is not the only capitalist super-power. There are many others, including of course the EEC. They have all apparently given up their colonialist mentality. But this has been replaced by a neo-colonialist mentality.

Others do not see communism as the cause of evil. For them the world's evil is caused by economic alliances—represented by huge supra-national combines —and political, military and technological alliances.

These combines control the world and exacerbate the difference in wealth between the developed and the under-developed countries. Many people who are aware of this situation feel despairingly that only armed violence can fight so powerful an enemy.

It is true that both communism and these combines are gaining so strong a grasp on the world that there is nothing to choose between them.

Armed violence claims to be the politically realistic solution, but this is not true. What can weapons stolen from army barracks or bought with money obtained by holding up banks do against an enemy whose allies are the manufacturers of the most modern and powerful weapons of extermination? . . .

Let it not be thought that I am moralising when I say that the chief difficulty in the task of changing the structures in both developed and under-developed countries, in both capitalist and socialist countries, is selfishness. It is selfishness which makes the rich in poor countries shut their eyes to the inhuman conditions suffered by their fellow countrymen. They refuse to see and think of themselves as good humane people, although they are responsible for these conditions. It is selfishness which makes the rich in rich countries refuse likewise to recognise the pockets of dire poverty which exist even in their countries. And above all selfishness prevents people from recognising the effects on poor countries of the unjust terms of international trade.

Let us make no mistake. Selfishness is not confined to one group or country. It is universal. If certain under-developed countries succeeded in becoming developed, their selfishness could easily lead them to behave in exactly the same way towards countries which still remained poor, as the rich countries disgusted them by behaving before.

We know that when workers manage to reach a decent standard of living after terrific struggles, they are tempted to forget about people who remain in misery both at home and in the under-developed countries.

The true root of evil is selfishness. Mankind can only get out of its present explosive situation when it realises that selfishness is international. It dominates the relationships between individuals, groups and countries.

Selfishness must be resisted actively and intelligently first of all within each one of us.

God's school

Give all you have.
Give all you are.
Give yourself always
unstintingly.
Joy and peace
to those who love the earth
and they receive
God, three persons who share
and are fulfilled in unity.

33

Lord, try us

There are those
whose being
is possession.
There are those
whose essence
is giving.

2 Marginalisation: a universal phenomenon

Anyone who has stood by the road trying to hitch a lift
in a hurry and watched the motor cars flash past him,
can understand what is meant by 'marginal'.

A marginal person is someone who is left by the
wayside in the economic, social, political and cultural
life of his country.

We could imagine that in an under-developed country the whole population would be living in the same
sub-human conditions. But this is not the case. What
usually happens might be called an internal colonialism. Small groups of rich people live off the poverty of
their fellow citizens. These small local rich groups help
the great rich foreigners. Some call them a 'consular
bourgeoisie' because they are like the consuls who used
to be sent abroad to represent an empire or an emper-
or.

We could imagine that there are no marginal persons
in developed countries. This is also false. Even in rich
countries there are groups who remain poor. Remain
marginal.

They might be immigrants who have come to look
for work, old-age pensioners, the unemployed.

Marginalisation does not only affect groups or individuals. There exist today marginal countries or even continents. This is what we mean by the 'third world', Africa, Asia and Latin America.

The first development decade has come and gone. The rich countries have become richer and the poor countries have become poorer. Marginalisation has increased.

The problem is more complicated than that because marginalisation has at least three stages. At the first stage the marginal do not reap the benefits of economic progress. At the second stage they are deprived of productive power. At the third stage they are deprived of the power of decision.

Economic benefits are not enough for anyone. If men do not share consciously in the process of the creation of wealth, and particularly in the choice of development model, if they share in no decision-making, they will only receive crumbs from a paternalist table.

With the progress of technology governments are led to employ increasingly highly qualified technicians, whom they equip and pay generously. It is they who draw up statistics, enquiries etc. to determine development models, and the ends and means necessary for governments to set them up.

There are people who calmly say that it is impossible to allow non-specialists to become mixed up in development plans. There are people who believe in the need for strong government, governments which dispense with parliament or maintain it simply as a rubber stamp, who control the universities and prevent the students from making any effective protest against plans drawn up by technocrats, who control the press and force it to give the official line instead of allowing it its proper freedom to criticise . . .

On the eve of the twenty-first century will man renounce his intelligence and his freedom? Will he allow
others to think and make decisions for him?

Put your ear to the ground

Put your ear to the ground
and listen,
hurried, worried footsteps,
bitterness, rebellion.
Hope
hasn't yet begun.
Listen again.
Put out feelers.
The Lord is there.
He is far less likely
to abandon us
in hardship
than in times of ease.

3 Education for freedom or slavery?

If we want to understand the situation we must ask the
fundamental question, has the education which has
formed our world given us freedom or made us slaves?

We must judge the tree by its fruits. We see clearly
that the education given by families, schools, churches,
small and great religions, needs many changes.

Parents may want the best for their children, schools
may claim to educate for life, the church teaches the
fatherhood of God and the brotherhood of man. The
result of all these efforts is that 20 per cent of mankind
owns more than 80 per cent of the resources and 80 per

cent has only 20 per cent of the world's resources on which to live.

We are told that man is about to gain control over matter and that science can promise wonders. We may give as examples: the achievements and future possibilities of industrial chemistry, the achievements of space travel, the achievements of medicine in controlling endemic diseases, and curing diseases previously thought to be incurable—will they soon be able to create life in the laboratory or abolish death?—the achievements of bio-chemistry in agriculture and the conquest of the depths of the sea, modern means of transport and communication and their future possibilities . . . This list, which it would be easy to add to, proves (or does it?) the triumphant achievement of education.

We should not be afraid of progress. Man has only just begun to accomplish what he was created for; he was commanded by God to subdue the earth and finish the work of creation. We should not deny the positive and glorious achievements of mankind. But if we believe that the truth will make us free, we must see that much of what passes for education is not concerned with the truth because it has not succeeded in freeing us. It is vital that we should unite in support of a liberating education. This is the fundamental task for the Abrahamic minorities.

A liberating education would be based on certain principles:

Every man is responsible through what he does and what he fails to do for the destiny of mankind.

For the judaeo-christian religions, the basic truth is the biblical teaching that God made man in his own image.

Individualism causes selfishness, the root of all evil.

37

Having and *being* go together; they are complementary and the one cannot be without the other.

Evil is not having. We should not be afraid of what men's genius might invent. But what we must do is make sure that progress does not only benefit more and more restricted groups. It should be for the good of all mankind. Poverty makes people sub-human. Excess of wealth makes people inhuman.

War is daily becoming more absurd. It is literally true that it could be the collective suicide of mankind. But as well as nuclear warfare and biological warfare we also have poverty, the most bloody, evil and shameful war of them all.

There is urgent work to be done: We must free technology from the exclusive control of governments and big business and place it at the service of all mankind. We must completely rethink military service because war has become meaningless and the only possible war today is the war we must fight against underdevelopment and misery. Education will fail as long as there are dictatorships on the right or the left.

We must put an end to violence. To do this we must have the courage to recognise the source of all violence and put an end to injustice everywhere. Poor countries suffer from internal colonialism and neo-colonialism; rich countries allow groups of poor people to remain within them and the rich have become inhuman through an excess of comfort and luxury. It is easy to show that the wealth of the rich countries is sustained by the misery of the poor countries. We must end all this injustice. The scandal of this century is marginalisation, which deprives two-thirds of humanity of progress, the power to create wealth or make their own decisions.

The young are very important. We must be brave

38

enough to trust them, really talk with them and accept their demands for authenticity and justice, and at the same time have enough moral force to require them to respect authenticity and justice.

Atheists and christians should revise their views of each other. Belief in God does not necessarily make men slaves. Many atheists can share the belief in man as co-creator. In any case education for freedom cannot do without the help of atheists, and christians should realise that atheist humanism shows an effective love for mankind.

Religions are uniting to show that love of men is a special way of loving God. They are trying to preach the gospel both to the poor who have been made subhuman by their living conditions, so that they may know the truth which will help them get rid of their poverty, and to the rich, who have become inhuman through their excesses, so that they may know the truth which will help them become human again. They try to denounce selfishness as the great evil and unmask it at the local, regional, national and international levels.

It is urgent that we should all unite to denounce and overcome fear. Those who have nothing fear they can do nothing about it, those who have much fear that their goods will be taken away from them.

The basis of education is genuine respect for the human person. Mutual respect between husband and wife, to help each other to go on growing; the respect due to every child because he is a unique human being; respect by those in authority for their office so that they do not abuse it; respect by those under authority, so that they can take orders without becoming servile.

What then should education free us from? From selfishness which leads to pride, closes men in, and causes unhappiness, tension, division, separation in families, groups, parties and even religions. Selfishness which has grown to global dimensions and makes solidarity and real peace between men impossible.

Teach your child from infancy

Teach your child from infancy
to love open spaces,
widen his mind.
He will be glad of this,
especially if later
he must endure
a life confined
by a slit window's littleness
to one small patch of sky.

Truth is alive and suffering

It is as important
to free the truth
from systems of thought
which suffocate it,
as it is to free men
from inhuman
imprisonment
to the death.

4 Hesitations to be overcome

The more we have to lose, the more weighty becomes our decision to respond to God's call, and the more fiercely and subtly we resist. 'It's not sensible to carry what may be just an impulse too far.' 'The structures which have been built up over centuries cannot and should not be changed in a few hours or even days, weeks or years . . ."

There are sincere and respectable persons who are the first to advise moderation in all things. 'Because only agitators and hence communists will benefit from any exaggeration, rush or radicalisation.'

We must see clearly and educate our conscience so that we are not overcome by the temptations offered by ourselves or others. We should not be overawed by the need to maintain public order. Let us examine this public order. It is no exaggeration to say that it is not order but established disorder.

We should not be frightened of communist infiltration. The danger of communism will become imminent if we have not the courage to attack structures of slavery and if people continue to call anyone a communist who demands social justice, even if he is manifestly anti-communist. Let us not forget that while people are dying in the name of communism or anti-communism, the capitalist and communist empires are perfectly able to agree when their interests demand it.

We must go beyond 'aid' or 'charity' and demand justice which will bring peace. Many people falter at this point. He who asks the powerful to give aid to the poor, or helps the poor himself by being imprudent enough, or bold enough, to mention these or those rights or demand this or that justice, is regarded as a splendid man, a saint. But he who chooses to demand justice generally, seeking to change structures that reduce millions of God's children to slavery, must expect his words to be distorted, to be libelled and slandered, viewed with disfavour by governments, perhaps imprisoned, tortured, killed . . . But this is the eighth beatitude: 'Blessed are you when men revile you and persecute you and utter all kinds of evil against you falsely

41

on my account. Rejoice and be glad for your reward is great in heaven, for so men persecuted the prophets who were before you.' But is there any point in a peaceful demand for justice, even if this peaceful demand is firm and determined, when we are bound up and compromised in our daily life by the whole structure of injustice and oppression?

To the extent that we genuinely admit the contradiction, to the extent that we truly want to find the way out both for ourselves and the institutions to which we belong, it is an excellent thing to become involved on the side of truth and justice.

An enormous effort will be needed to create awareness in the marginalised masses, both in the developed and the under-developed countries, to prepare them to fight their way out of their sub-human situation, and also prepare them not simply to become as bourgeois and as selfish as those whom today they condemn.

An enormous effort is also needed to create awareness in those who are privileged, both in rich countries where there are poor groups which they allow to remain, and there is neo-colonialism which they support whether they realise it or not, and in under-developed countries where the privileged create and profit from internal colonialism. It is very difficult to create awareness in the privileged. The teacher must have great virtue, be kind but truthful, gentle but firm.

But if the effort is not made the scandal will continue and the rich will go on getting richer and the poor poorer. The spiral of violence will get worse, injustice will increase, the resistance of the oppressed or the young in the name of the oppressed will continue and repression will become more and more brutal.

When will governments and the privileged understand that there can be no true peace until justice has been established?

Go down

Go down
into the plans of God.
Go down
deep as you may.
Fear not
for your fragility
under that weight of water.
Fear not
for life or limb
sharks attack savagely.
Fear not the power
of treacherous currents under the sea.
Simply, do not be afraid.
Let go. You will be led
like a child whose mother
holds him to her bosom
and against all comers is his shelter.

5 Are institutions hopeless?

One of the temptations that face the Abrahamic minorities is the fear that the structures of which they are part make it impossible for them to have any real effect in changing the world. They are tempted because they do not feel they are better than other people.

For example priests or nuns who want to follow the spirit of Vatican II or bring into effect the conclusions of the Latin American bishops' conference at Medellin should not be astonished if they feel misunderstood by their brothers and sisters. They would be yielding to temptation if they decided to leave their community and give way to dangerous bitterness.

Instead of feeling beaten, instead of quitting and imagining how to reform the institution from the outside, would it not be better to think that within the institution itself and in all sorts of places there are others who are in the middle of the very same experience? Why not seek an intelligent and effective way, which would also be loyal and constructive, of contacting all these others who are also anxious to serve their neighbour better? I do not mean condemning those who are more conservative or plotting against them. I mean you need not feel isolated, you need not be discouraged, when you are trying to revitalise the institution itself from within.

Of course you will risk being misunderstood. However pure your intentions you will look like a rebel. Perhaps you will be punished. This is excellent training for attacking and overcoming socio-economic and politico-cultural structures. You will be able to take the measure of your courage, prudence, loyalty, kindness, power of decision and responsibility.

Similar situations also arise in the protestant churches. Protestants following the gospel and the conclusions of the Uppsala or Bayreuth congresses, and wanting to bring peace through justice and work for a true education for freedom, may also feel hampered. People are shocked and suspicious of them. They are regarded as 'advanced' or even 'crypto-communist'. They think that these judgments on them are against the gospel. They are scandalised and angry and think they will have to leave their church in order to remain faithful to Christ.

Many clergy and lay people are likewise tempted. However right and necessary it is to attack the faults of these institutions, it is a grave mistake to think they can simply be wiped out for a fresh start to be made. It is impossible to live outside a minimum structure or organisation. Unfortunately even those structures which are most effective and reasonable to begin with always become intolerable after a while.

Everyone should realise that there are other young people, and adults, everywhere who want what they want . . . Minorities in every group could form a nucleus for the greater service of others and all these minorities united could become an irresistible force.

Young buddhists, shintoists, moslems, jews, catholics and atheists all have the same reactions today to their own structures. This advice is for all of them: be aware of the temptation and take steps to overcome it.

Other structures also repress instead of encouraging initiative. Doctors and nurses are sometimes deprived of the most basic equipment for their work. Teachers sometimes have nowhere for their pupils to sit. Social workers spend time working out large projects but are not given the means even to put small projects into practice. All these people should realise that they are not alone in their desire to serve their neighbour more effectively. There are minorities everywhere with the same desire. It would be easy to give further examples, among workers, peasants, journalists, soldiers etc. . . . There are Abrahamic minorities everywhere who are only waiting for the signal to begin and to unite.

So you think that

So you think that
because of her weaknesses,
Christ will forsake her?
The worse his church and ours
is marred by our failures,
the steadier he will support her
with his tender care.
He could not deny
his own body.

The harmonist

I admire and envy
your rare ear,
true to each note
discerning falsity
however slight.
And even more
your mastery,
blending the dissonant
into harmony.

3

ABRAHAMIC MINORITIES UNITE!

1 The violence of the truth

If you feel you belong in spirit to the family of Abraham do not wait for permission to act. Don't wait for official action or new laws. The family of Abraham is more a spirit than an institution, more a life style than an organisation. It requires the minimum of structure and refers merely to several general principles.

The minimum of structure: anyone who feels he belongs to the family of Abraham should not remain alone. Make an effort to find someone, near at hand or further away, who already belongs to this family or who could belong. Make contact. How? That depends on the situation. The essential thing is to get out of isolation. There are no rules about the formation of groups, number of members, form that meetings should take. You are brothers meeting to help each other fight discouragement, and develop the necessary faith, hope and love.

The first thing to do is to look and listen, get information on the situations in which the Abrahamic minorities could be involved. Won't that be a big job? No. Any member of the Abrahamic minorities can find out about what is happening around him, in the neighbourhood where he lives or at work.

He must discover where the worst injustices are, the worst exhibitions of selfishness, from the local to the international scale. Every member of the family of Abraham, according to his opportunities, will be able to get much more detailed and human information than can be gathered from the official statistics.

In under-developed countries the Abrahamic minorities must try to find out and understand what is involved in a sub-human situation. 'Sub-human' is an explosive word. Take it in detail. Find out about housing. Do the places where some people live deserve to be called houses? Do they afford the necessary minimum of comfort to a human life? How many people are there per room? Look at the water, drains, electricity, the floor, the roof. Investigate clothing, food, health, work, transport, leisure in the same way. Pictures can be helpful. Take photographs and so on. But you must also turn to statistics to discover whether this is an isolated case or the general condition. You should ask the right questions. With work, for example, does it pay a living wage sufficient to support a family, is employment guaranteed or are there frequent redundancies? Are trade unions encouraged, tolerated, interfered with, forbidden? What are the apprenticeship conditions? the sanitary conditions? holidays? retirement provisions? Are the laws on social conditions kept? Are human beings treated with respect?

This sort of inquiry could of course arouse suspicion, and that could have unpleasant consequences. But it is necessary to find out what the real situation is in conditions of internal colonialism.

What other way is there of becoming convinced and of convincing others of the huge gap between those who operate and those who suffer from an almost feudal situation in which the masses have no voice and no hope? Such information would not aim at inciting anger and rebellion but at providing a solid argument for the necessity to change the structures.

We should not forget the extreme cases where it would be necessary to prove that an apparently patriarchal regime is in fact a cover for absolute dominion over life and death, for a master who can give and take at will, allow or forbid the provision and maintenance of houses, the cultivation of a small strip of land and the keeping of a few cattle, literacy, trade unionism etc.

How are we to find out about the price paid by sweated workers, slaves innumerable, for profits to those who put their money in foreign banks in secret numbered accounts?

How can we find out about abuses of economic power on the national and international scale? Where can we find figures for what official statistics do not disclose, for the illegal export of profits that are blood, sweat and tears?

Must we repeat it? Such information does not aim to provoke hatred or subversion. Its aim is to supply liberating moral pressure. For many, this in itself is dangerous and subversive. But one day it will be understood that this violence of the peaceful is greatly preferable to the explosion of armed violence.

In developed countries the Abrahamic minorities must also investigate and try to understand, for example:

The existence of under-development (grey zones) in rich countries, and what this means in terms of human misery.

The injustices in trade between developed and under-developed countries.

The difference between the aid figures for poor

countries and the figures for the losses made by these countries because the price of primary materials is kept so low that they cannot pay for the manufactured goods they have to buy.

The inhuman and criminal sale or gift of arms to poor countries under the pretext that these aid development, and which involve these poor countries in dangerous and ridiculous arms races and increase local poverty.

Details of the reality of economic power . . .

It would be humiliating to admit that one was unable to gather such information. The challenge must be accepted.

Choosing the way of moral pressure is not choosing the easy way out. We are replacing the force of arms by moral force, the violence of the truth. We must believe that love can strengthen the courage and the numbers of these Abrahamic minorities who want justice but who refuse to answer violence with violence.

Love will find the way to rouse and organise these minorities in all human groups.

Love will find the best way to unite without uniformity these various non-violent movements so that they can help each other.

Love will enable them to find in their religion or even in atheist humanism steadfastness in the fight for the peaceful liberation of oppressed peoples all over the world, whatever the consequences.

Love will help them to decide firmly that the goal is not superficial reform but the transformation of inhuman structures, to find methods which although they are non-violent are useful and effective in bringing about this transformation.

In their work of diagnosing unjust situations, in their

action of liberating moral pressure these minorities must be careful to remain humble. As we know our own selfishness, we must be aware that if we were in the place of those we condemn, we might behave in the same way as they do. Our family, our group or church may also bear some of the responsibility for those situations which we have decided peacefully but decisively to change.

Join together

Stone, brick and tile
together all
compose
the house.
Unbuilt the pile
of single elements
are the hope
of a house.
But more important
is to plan and put it up.
The building done
is greater than
the unassembled material.

2 Anonymous heroism

Forgive me if I disturb your peace of mind. But why not ask yourself today, without wasting time deciding whether you have received little or much, whether you have been given the wonderful but awkward, great but dangerous vocation to serve humanity as a member of the Abrahamic minorities?

51

If we are to understand the potential force of these minorities, we must realise the value of each man however 'average' he may be. It would be easy to discount such a man, who is neither a great saint nor a great sinner, incapable either of great cowardice or courage. He wants to live in peace with his own family. We are tempted to apply to him the terrible words of the bible: he is neither cold nor hot. God will spew him out of his mouth.

If it is true that the average man is not made for heroism or martyrdom, it is also true that his daily life is made up of sacrifices and acts of anonymous heroism.

The taxi driver in a small provincial town who provides for the education of his eight children. The clerical worker's wife who performs miracles of organisation to add to her husband's salary what they need for their two children and the third one on the way. The girl who does not marry but adopts eleven nephews, who are the children of her two brothers . . . In the Middle Ages this was called 'white martyrdom'. We could give endless examples of it.

These are the people whose sacrifice is their daily grind. Are there others who could take on the problems of the larger human family? The average man lives monotonously—the same house, the same faces, the same voices, the same worries—these others give themselves without stint. They accept the burden and they do not remain anonymous.

It would be stupid and unjust to despise the average man, who is after all in the majority. We should try to form an alliance between him and the front-line fighters. We should recognise, truly not just as a tactical manoeuvre, the value of anonymous heroism, white martyrdom.

If we give him his due, the average man will readily see for his part that others might have a different vocation, and see also that there might be ways in which he could help the work of these minorities. If he is understood, informed, listened to and roused to peaceful violence, this average man could play a vital part.

Its own function

Bolt and nut
are as essential
in the job they do
as a head of state
to avert evil.
Both fail too.

Do not forget

In a fabulous
necklace
I had to admire
the anonymous string
by which the whole thing
was strung together.

3 Two particular appeals

There is a risk of sounding disagreeable in making distinctions between classes of readers. To mention some and leave out others could cause resentment, even if it was unintentional. In this chapter two particular appeals are made and an even more particular appeal in the next. We are not trying to slight anyone by omission or make unfavourable comparisons.

It is impossible to list all the groups that could be helpful and we are simply taking three groups of whom much can be hoped. Of course we could appeal to other groups too. I cheerfully admit and support these too, in advance.

To artists

The artist cannot be judged by the measure of ordinary mortals. He shares more directly in the creating power of the Father. Everything in him is unexpected and original. He bridles against regulation, monotony, routine.

The artist is usually open to the human values of justice and freedom. He cannot breathe the air of dictatorship. He is ultra sensitive and feels the coming future. He speaks (each in his proper language, poetry, theatre, cinema, painting, sculpture, music) in the name of others who cannot speak.

By definition artists belong to the Abrahamic minorities. If an artist does not care about the construction of a more human world, he must have become bourgeois and sold to avarice, ambition and selfishness.

What can be expected from committed artists in the Abrahamic minorities? They should be so thoroughly aware of the great problems facing mankind and the greatest injustices that it automatically comes out in their work.

Poets helped to condemn black slavery. Poets, slavery still goes on! More than two thirds of mankind are slaves to hunger, sickness, forced labour, despair. And the other third is in slavery to selfishness and fear.

Popular music bears the message further than the

most learned scientific treatises. What the people sing speaks to the mind and imagination of both singer and listener.

Theatre has been and always will be powerful. It is indispensable for the work of making people more aware of the situation, particularly if it reaches the common people.

The cinema is the medium with the greatest impact on the masses because it is pictorial. Good documentaries can have great power.

Humour is a subtle and effective instrument. There are situations where in practice there is nothing to be done but make people laugh and the oppressors often do not understand what the laughter is about . . .

We could continue this list. What is essential is that the artist should be a genuine artist. He should not be a mere propagandist. That would debase his work. His message should be flesh of his flesh and blood of his blood.

The Judgment

When on judgment day
the angels call the artists in,
they will be so proud
of their share
in God the Father's power
of creation,
that the Son
will find it hard
to judge them strictly,
because poets especially
remind him of his Father.

To atheist humanists

Not long ago people wondered whether atheists could
really exist. How would it be possible for the creature
to do without God? Isn't atheism simply snobbery
which vanishes in a crisis? In the oft quoted phrase, 'I
am an atheist, thank God.' But today there can be no
doubt that atheists exist throughout the world. There
are people who do not believe in God for the simple
reason that they feel no need of him, either in their
thoughts or their actions, their private or public life,
their easy or their hard times.

This calm atheism is much more serious than the
old-fashioned militant and aggressive kind, which often
sounded like bitter resentment of God. We often hear
of the death of God. For many the expression simply
means the death of a concept of God made in the
image and likeness of men. As our idea of God becomes purer the simple faith of the child must grow

into the more enlightened vision of the adult. Those who reject God in the name of science may one day discover that the mind can seek outside the boundaries of science without betraying itself. Those who get rid of God because they consider him incompatible with the freedom of man may one day see that it is possible to think of man as a co-creator who is able to free himself from slavery.

We do not want to argue about the existence of God here. We see that there are men who are atheists who are also humanists and concerned with the human person, liberation and development. A believer might say that the phrase 'atheistic humanism' is sort of double atheism. It both denies the existence of God and puts man in the place of God. But those who have anything to do with humanists realise that this is not the case. For the believer the law is to love God and his neighbour. Anyone who loves his neighbour is already fulfilling half the law. Anyone who truly loves his neighbour must also love, without knowing it, the creator and Father.

We all know that people, often young people, become atheists because believers, particularly believers in positions of responsibility, disappoint them when they do not practice what they preach.

Some atheist humanists are very impressive. They love truth, justice and peace, they are willing to serve and give of their utmost, they are brave and resist suffering and torture; they are examples to the believer.

We who are believers can say that any man who lives the truth and who has the courage to work for peace in this way, will see God.

And in any case in the work of the Abrahamic minorities atheist humanists have a crucial part. They are usually respected not only by young atheists but also by believers who have their doubts and problems. An atheist humanist can be of the greatest help to the Abrahamic minorities. He can give an example of the gift of his time and reputation for the cause of justice on the way to peace. He can rouse unbelievers or doubters to shake off their indifference and leave their ease to risk the construction of a better world. He can find in his very atheism reasons to convince himself and others why they should become involved in the struggle against injustice, marginalisation and slavery.

In te speravi semper

This speaker
was not born within your fold,
supported by your grace,
held fast, never
to turn from you his face.

Hear the voice
of those who in all honesty
feel bound to choose
the cold
outside your house.

Nevertheless,
they still believe in you,
although they may not know it,
for are not you the truth?
And these people both
speak it and (in your own phrase)
do it.

You are beauty
and pure eyes remaining childlike
still look
wonderingly
on your earth's loveliness.

You are goodness
and I find
you in people who do not confess
you. They lack your body
but speak your mind.

4 A very particular appeal

I make this very particular appeal to the young. It is not difficult to understand why. Later the young people of today will be better understood than they are. Their splendid values will be acknowledged and their faults will be seen as partly caused by us adults. Before we make this appeal to the young, let us try and understand them.

Let us try and see this young man sleeping in the airport lounge at Los Angeles. He is a North American. He has just come back from Vietnam. The untidy uniform betrays that this adolescent is not a born soldier. He was taken from university and had a machine gun put into his hands. He was sent half bewildered to Vietnam and forced to kill in order not to be killed. With total repugnance he must have pulled the trigger and killed for no reason young men like himself.

How can we be surprised if he turned to drugs to deaden his feelings? . . . He has come back from an absurd war—and what war is not absurd?—and he has not been welcomed with flowers. Nearly everyone looks at him with a sort of contemptuous pity. His girlfriend does not want to see him any more. His younger brothers do not want to hear about his feats of war and laugh at his medals. His parents wonder how he can be got back into ordinary life . . .

Now try to imagine a room with dim lights in a country house. About twenty young men and women, knowing that in winter the house is left empty and shut up, have got hold of the key. The house belongs to one of the girls' parents. For three days and nights they smoke and try to dance, smoke and try to talk, smoke and try to get excited. Suddenly the owner of the house appears and finds them sitting, crashed out or asleep, their eyes closed or open and staring wildly. She had intended to throw them out and force her daughter to come home with her. But the sight is so painful that she dare not throw any of them out. She is overcome and sits on the ground among these young people in distress and bursts into tears.

If they dared speak, of course none of them could justify their suicidal behaviour. But they would all make clear that they did not just smoke for the sake of smoking. They feel what seems to them the absurdity of life. They find no cause worthy of their youth and strength and they try to forget them.

It would be easy to give more examples. We could also mention young people, some almost children, who lose patience and engage in armed struggle. But as well as this, everywhere, in both rich and poor countries, there are many extraordinary young people, full of hope and generosity, ready to give all that they value most to build a better world.

Young men and women, the world is also young. The Abrahamic minorities are open to all, but you have a special place in them.

Let every word

Let every word
be the fruit
of action and reflection.
Reflection alone
without action
or tending towards it
is mere theory,
adding its weight
when we are
overloaded
with it already
and it has led
the young to despair.
Action alone
without reflection
is being busy
pointlessly.
Honour the Word eternal
and speak
to make
a new world possible.

5 The prayer of the family of Abraham

Some believe in and rely on prayer, others think of it as
mumbo jumbo. But we should not allow the word
prayer to divide us. Whenever we express our dearest
wishes, that is praying.

What prayer could the Abrahamic minorities say in
common, over and above their differences?

Let us open our eyes. Let us begin at once to fight

our selfishness and come out of ourselves, to dedicate ourselves once and for all, whatever the sacrifices, to the non-violent struggle for a juster and more human world.

Let us not put off the decision till tomorrow. Let us begin today, now, intelligently and firmly.

Let us look about us and recognise our brothers and sisters who are called like us to give up their ease and join all those who hunger for the truth and who have sworn to give their lives to make peace through justice and love.

Let us not waste time discussing who shall be our leader. What is important is for us to unite and go forward, remembering that time too is our enemy.

Let us give the best of ourselves to helping create moral pressure for freedom to bring about the necessary structural changes.

Let us gather information on the situations we wish to change.

Let us spread this information by all reasonable means at our disposal. And let the information be truthful, able to stand up to criticism and disturb the consciences of all good men.

Let us through all this stand firm without falling into hatred, let us be understanding without conniving at evil.

Let us make our own the prayer of St. Francis of Assisi and let us give our lives to putting it into practice:

Lord make me an instrument of your peace.
Where there is hatred let me sow love.
Where there is resentment let me bring forgiveness.
Where there is discord let me bring harmony.
Where there is error let me bring truth.
Where there is doubt let me bring faith.
Where there is despair let me bring hope.
Where there is darkness let me bring light.
Where there is sadness let me bring joy.
Master, let me not seek
rather to be consoled than to console,
to be understood than to understand
to be loved than to love.
For
in giving we receive
in forgetting ourselves we find ourselves
in forgiving that we are forgiven
in dying that we rise to eternal life.